THE BACK HOME SERIES

Series Titles

Body Talk
Takwa Gordon

The In-Between State
Martha Lundin

North Freedom
Carolyn Dallmann

Ohio Apertures
Robert Miltner

Praise for
Takwa Gordon

Takwa Gordon's *Body Talk* is an artistic, poignant portrait of vulnerability, self love, and survival. Takwa not only takes you on her personal journey, but she also challenges the reader to look deep within their own mind and body. She reminds us all that the body really does communicate if only you can learn to listen to it. Her book will help you finally learn how. It is an essential read for anyone with a body. That is to say, it is a must read for *everyone*.

—Aitch Alexandar
author of *My Body is a Junkyard*

I believe that the goal of poetry and prose should be not to impress with rhyme and wordplay but to punch the reader square in the face, and to challenge their perceptions by giving them the opportunity to see the world through someone else's eyes. When it's done well, this kind of writing has the power to transform, and Takwa Gordon's *Body Talk* does just that. It is at once an unflinching study of abuse and trauma, an illuminating meditation on the impact of racism and religious bigotry, and an uplifting chronicle of recovery and empowerment.

—Vince Font
Author and Owner/Editor of Glass Spider Publishing

In her hybrid memoir, *Body Talk*, Somali-American writer Takwa Gordon recounts her burning personal experiences in the diaspora and back home. Gruesome episodes of childhood and grisly amounts of adulthood experienced in Africa and America are painfully presented both in prose and poetry to arbitrate a past Self with a present Self. Anyone who has experienced armed conflicts in Africa or elsewhere may benefit from reading this memoir. The themes and issues (like the body and its memories) dramatized inwardly and outwardly by Takwa are the same and similar to those commonly encountered on a daily basis by everyone who fled from war.

—Mohamed Haji Ingiriis
Author of *The Suicidal State in Somalia*

Takwa Gordon's hybrid memoir seethes with raw pain that is both palpable and anguished. Yet the words she employs are measured, balanced, forward-looking. These are words that are not designed to draw blood, but to cure, mend, and heal impaled bodies and broken spirits. Gordon's aim is to reconcile with herself, allowing her to move forward. The memoir is framed by an African adage: *Life is in trust with you; run, run for your life*. The kind of running implied here is not hamstrung by fear and confusion; rather, it wrestles with life's vagaries and vicissitudes. The memoir also attests to the veracity of a Somali adage: *Elegy is the voice of the survivor*. Here is a voice that exudes a zest for life imbued by exuberant hope.

—Ali Jimale Ahmed
Queens College, CUNY

Witness Takwa Gordon turn suffering into resilience. "You are growing in ways that you just don't understand right now," she says. She has earned our trust by eschewing toxic positivity and reclaiming her own power from a world of the saved and the saviors. Sit through the storms in her honest company. Be refreshed by her friendship in the fierceness of this weather. Takwa insists that we can choose not to be fractured by it. Our wholeness is inherent. A love radical enough to include ourselves, her first and last lesson.

—Nan Seymour
Poet and Founder of River Writing

Body Talk

a hybrid memoir by

Takwa Gordon

Cornerstone Press
Stevens Point, Wisconsin

Cornerstone Press, Stevens Point, Wisconsin 54481
Copyright © 2022 Takwa Gordon
Illustrations © 2022 Takwa Gordon
www.uwsp.edu/cornerstone

Printed in the United States of America by
Point Print and Design Studio, Stevens Point, Wisconsin 54481

Library of Congress Control Number: 2022933509
ISBN: 978-1-7377390-8-1

All rights reserved.

This is a work of creative nonfiction. All of the events in this book are true to the best of the author's memory. Some names and identifying features have been changed to protect the identity of certain parties. The author in no way represents any company, corporation, or brand, mentioned herein. The views expressed in this memoir are solely those of the author.

Excerpt(s) from *Refuge: An Unnatural History of Family and Place* by Terry Tempest Williams, copyright © 1991 by Terry Tempest Williams. Used by permission of Pantheon Books, an imprint of the Knopf Doubleday Publishing Group, a division of Penguin Random House LLC. All rights reserved.

Cornerstone Press titles are produced in courses and internships offered by the Department of English at the University of Wisconsin–Stevens Point.

DIRECTOR & PUBLISHER   EXECUTIVE EDITOR
Dr. Ross K. Tangedal   Jeff Snowbarger

SENIOR EDITORS
Lexie Neeley, Monica Swinick, Kala Buttke

SENIOR PRESS ASSISTANT
Gavrielle McClung

PRESS STAFF
Rhiley Block, Alyssa Bronk, Grace Dahl, Patrick Fogarty, Ava Freeman, Kyra Goedken, Angela Green, Brett Hill, Cale Jacoby, Hunter Kiesow, Adam King, Jeremy Kremser, Amanda Leibham, Leo McEvilly, Annika Rice, Abbi Rohde, Abbi Wasielewski, Bethany Webb

This book is dedicated to all those who inhabit the borderlands.

And for those who have had to lean into curiosity, joy, and adventure, so that they could leave behind powerlessness and marginalization.

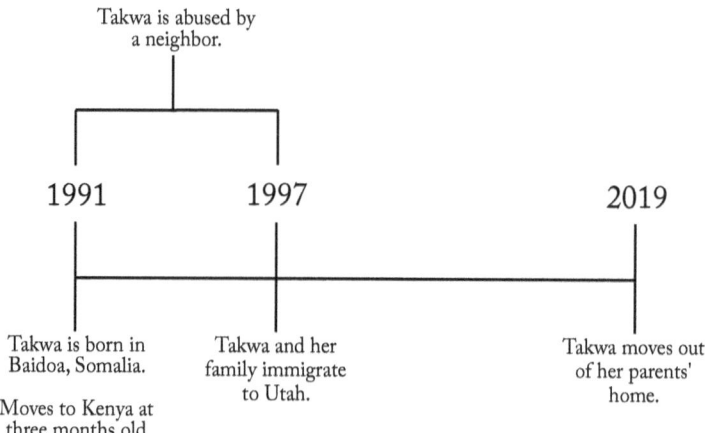

Contents

The Body and Its Memories 1

Love 33

Letters from My Partner 71

Notes 75
Bibliography 77
Acknowledgments 79

If you hear the dogs, keep going. If you see the torches in the woods, keep going. If there's shouting after you, keep going. Don't ever stop. Keep going. If you want a taste of freedom, keep going.

–attributed to Harriet Tubman

The Body and Its Memories

Be like the flower that gives its fragrance to even the hand that crushes it.

—attributed to Imam Ali ibn Abi Talib

The Disruption Caused by Trauma

I was a sophomore in college when I first read *The Inner Chapters* by the Chinese Daoist philosopher Chuang Tzu. In his book, Chuang Tzu explores how the body can experience emotions and states such as disassociation. Chuang Tzu repeatedly reminds the reader that there's no real separation between you and the Other. The Other is only in existence because of you, your mind, and language. Likewise, our identities and sense of self are rooted in the Other, e.g. "I am Black, and they are White."

At that time, I wasn't aware of why the concept of the Other and of disassociation were so important to me. Now, as I am fully aware of my history as a survivor of various traumatic experiences, I can see how this concept of the Other and detachment comes up in the form of disassociation.

In *What Happened to You?*, a book written on trauma, Dr. Bruce D. Perry and Oprah Winfrey define how disassociation works in survivors of trauma. Dr. Perry explains: "You [the trauma survivor] disengage from the external world and psychologically flee into your inner world" (59). They explain why this happens, "A key part of that sensitized ability to dissociate is to be a people-pleaser. You comply with what others want. You find yourself doing things to avoid conflict […] as well as gravitating toward various regulating, but dissociative, activities" (59).

In my life, disassociation's underlying causes of needing to please other people and avoid conflict would manifest in different ways: 1) I felt the need to constantly overachieve in every area of my life, especially in education; 2) I didn't have clear boundaries and would allow others, especially male relatives to define what I could and couldn't do. For example, I constantly turned down opportunities to present and travel because I was not allowed to by my very conservative father; 3) I also didn't have strong boundaries because I didn't want to be seen as difficult and rebellious.

Going back to Chuang Tzu's exploration of detachment and how we create the concept of the Self and the Other, the trauma that I experienced shaped my relationship with my body. Specifically, for me, the trauma and its effects shaped what it means to be a woman; it also shaped what it means to be both Black and Arab. My concept of Self and Other were also shaped by my healing journey.

This book, then, is my exploration of Blackness, Arabness, femininity and the female, as well as my desire to finally acknowledge the trauma that I experienced as a child and adult. I do this through poems, small snapshots from my memory, illustrations, and personal essays in the hopes of bridging the gaps between experiential, spiritual, and scientific. Most importantly, I want to heal the disruption caused by trauma for survivors of trauma: the body and mind are not separate. They are integrated.

One way to integrate the mind and body is by recognizing that our bodies hold memories. That is, like Chuang Tzu says, the body never forgets. This idea that there are body memories is apparent in books like *The Body Keeps the Score* by Dr. Bessel van der Kolk. In his book, van der Kolk shows how survivors of trauma tend to have bodily sensations or reactions because of trauma. That is, the body learns to *save* traumatic memories. These traumatic memories can be triggered by different sensory experiences like sight, smell, touch, and so much more.[1]

Think about it. What sights, smiles, textures, and sounds come to your mind when you think of your childhood or past? How does your body react to these memories? Do you feel soothed, calm, or happy as in the case of memories that are healing? Or do you sometimes feel agitated, afraid, or even angry as in the case of traumatic memories? The fact that we can be soothed or triggered shows that it's not only the mind that saves memories; the body does this as well.

The challenge in accepting body memories is realizing that the body can communicate. For example, chronic fatigue or illness isn't simply a sign of laziness (associated with the body); it's also a sign of worrying or being anxious. That's because we're feeling, and the things we've experienced in our past also shows up in our present. What this suggests is that in trauma survivors' journey to healing ourselves, we must learn to integrate our minds and bodies. This is especially true since we've been taught to disassociate as a method to coping with trauma. That is, we will no longer accept being separate from ourselves and our world. We are whole, and we choose mindfulness and self-awareness over detachment and fragmentation.

your childhood

You carry your childhood like
ripe berries in the innermost part of your palms.

Finding Africa

Somedays, I rummage through my mind,
Looking for a scroll explaining my childhood in Africa.

Yet, when I emerge,
I see the snippets,
the scenes of
people knocking door to door on Eid collecting money in an *Imame*
of being taken shopping by my sister to buy a doll
using the money I had gotten,
of eating mangoes laced with salt and chili,
of the niece who died from malaria in the next room
in our crowded home.

Sexualized Bodies

He pushes my dress to the side,
I feel his gruff hand searching
deep inside me,
his beard grazing on my cheek,
as he asks,
how it feels.

My small hips thrust
in-tandem with the hand,
the hand that would grip me tight
in my nightmares,
those dreams punctured with lots of shadows,
running, and sweat.

The 90s

"In America, we'll have lots of candy and soda."
We talked amongst ourselves as the fervor grew stronger in our home.

"Swear on Allah",
my father asked us,
"That you'll listen to us when you go to America."

America, the land of chocolate, soda, pale people, Rambo, basketball, and Somalis who had gone bad.

Snapshot: The Departure and Arrival

"*Ma'salam!*",³ I said, leaving my Barbie doll underneath the bunk bed and running to catch the ride to the airport.

"Bring the doll with you!" my sister yelled from outside.

"No," I said, "I'll come back for her."

My five-year-old self had spent many months diligently saving money to buy this doll: I had saved money from Eid celebrations and from relatives who visited my family. But at that moment, I just knew that I would be back to get my doll.

My first memory of being in America is landing at the airport in New York and having an agent from the airport wave at me. We had just been allowed in because we had all the necessary shots and tests prior to arriving here. From there, we were taken to a hotel. This hotel didn't fail to live up to our fantasies: there was a red carpet and lots of well-polished granite, something that I was very unfamiliar with. We also had room service, which we were very delighted about.

Of course, there were many things that we had to get used to that first night. For example, my parents tried to turn the shower on for us, but they didn't know which knob was for "cold" and which was "hot." So, we had spent a considerable amount of time just playing with the knobs, until, like Goldilocks, we found the temperature to be just right. We also spent a lot of time just looking at the snow which had covered all of New York. It was beautiful and it was the type of weather that was made just for sleeping in under a blanket.

Handsy

You twisted my seven-year-old nipples,
laughed and then said,
"That's what I'll do every time you don't listen."

One day, the nipple-twisting became too much,
So, I ran to mom and cried.

"Your dad's just playing with you,"
she said and turned her face away.

Snapshot: The Shameful Pleasure

"She's in the bathroom doing bad things,"

I could hear one of my siblings telling my mother.

I had not shut the bathroom door because I didn't like being alone in there.

My mother ran into the bathroom, grabbed my prepubescent body, and pinched my thighs until I cried. Pinching the thighs of girls is very common in the family that I grew up in (and possibly in other Somali families) because it's a way of "limiting" the harshness of the method of discipline, while also providing the pain the child needs to feel.

"How many times have I told you to not do that?" she told me. Her face was contorted, and her eyes wouldn't budge as they scanned my body.

I knew that my mother didn't like it when I rubbed my bottom on furniture or on other things that I could find.

"The next time you do this, I'll rub chili peppers on your butt," my mother told me. "That's the only way that you'll stop."

At that age, I didn't understand why the pleasure I was feeling was such a "bad" thing. I had learned that rubbing myself on things could be pleasurable from the molestation. As I aged though, I quickly learned to hide the masturbation. I had, however, internalized the shame associated with masturbating.

Approval

I waited for your approval,
held countless grades and certificates as proof,
cleaned and made the home,
full of frankincense.

I accepted the taunts and stares,
of being from down south,
where borders touch,
where the sun has darkened,
this skin.

Becoming the Moon

I used to sit by the window every day,
peering at the girls next door,
always coming in and out.

When the blood first came,
You said,
"It's time that you realize
a face seen too many times
loses its beauty."

And that's how I came to my womanhood.

Learning

"*Abba*,"[4]
I said feeling embarrassed as the school secretary looked at me as I spoke in *May-May*,
"Everyone is going on a field trip.
The teacher said that I should call and ask you if I can go.
Can I go?"

"No,"
you said,
"Thank you for telling me."

Mixed Feelings

As the bus drove away and passed by our house,
your gray eyes sprang from behind the curtains,
your hands gently pulling the material to the side,
until your full form appeared.

You wave.
The kids in the bus stare.

"Picture-perfect,"
they say.

Cute. Maternal. A cultivator.

Snapshot: 9/11 and Racial Passing

"Go back to your country!" my neighbor's child screamed from the comfort of her mother's car. Their mom had just rolled the window down so that I could clearly hear what was being said. 9/11 had just happened and I had chosen to wear the *hijab* a year earlier so I could easily be identified as a Muslim, or for those who didn't know better, an Arab/South Asian.

When I told my parents about this incident and others that would follow, they asked my sisters and I, "Do you still want to wear the *hijab* knowing how dangerous it is in this political climate?" We said that we would like to continue wearing the *hijab*. After a few weeks, my parents decided that since I walked to school, I could no longer wear the *hijab* until things had died down.

But things didn't die down.

As a teenager and young adult, I came to see myself through the lens of others. A woman of the desert. The *hijabi* with sandy-brown skin. Rather than finding a mirror being held up to me, a clear reflection of who I thought I was, I instead saw blocks of brick, all with the words "brown" screaming back at me. Only as an adult in college would I learn that identity is a fleeting concept that's constantly being redefined personally and socially.[5]

Here I was, a biracial *Black* woman, being classified by my *hijab* as an Arab or South Asian. I did, indeed, have Arab blood, but so did many coastal East Africans. That is, how could I explain the sandy-brown skin of some East Africans? My mother's grayish-brown eyes? My siblings varying hair textures and complexions? The features that made me and my family the Other?

But I quickly learned that my experiences weren't unique—they spanned the various cultures of America.

The America of my childhood dreams wasn't just red carpets and room service, it was a place where people rolled down windows and hurled insults, a place where I would learn about myself and who the world thought I was.

The Awakening

I remember the first time I saw a slave ship,
the drawings of enslaved Africans chained together,
bodies stacked on top of each other,
so that if one felt like taking her life,
she would be taking everyone else with her.

I wept,
felt broken,
asked God, "How could you let this happen?"

Orientalism

They said
that
real women
like
Nancy Drew,
were women with
piercing blue eyes.

But me?
Women like me are
the mystery.

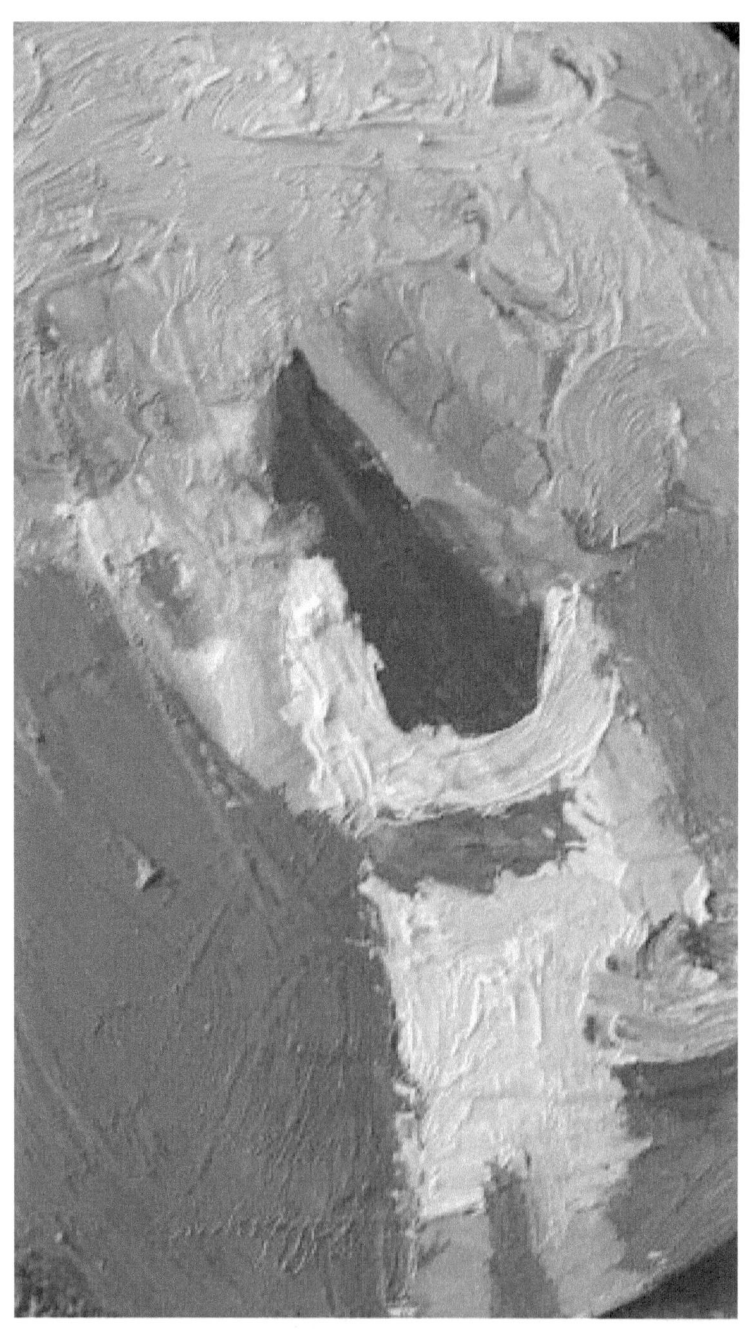

Shades

The nomadic Somali women who herd the livestock
following the rain,
as drought looms over this region.

The Somali metropolitan woman,
managing a business,
taking care of her family,
while living with PTSD.

Can we celebrate them,
as we do
Araweelo?[6]

Snapshot: The Kids at School

"You're not an Arab," my Arab best friend texted me.
"What?" I texted back, shocked.
"You're not an Arab," she repeated.
"I know," I said, "I just didn't like the way that they were making Arabs look. You don't need to be an Arab to speak up."

As time went by, I began to avoid sending pictures of myself to her. I was too worried that should she see my curly hair and my skin that gets darker during the summer—that she would see that I was indeed not an Arab.

Love

Once you learn to read, you will be forever free.
    —attributed to Frederick Douglass

The Path

> *Volunteers are beginning to reconstruct the marshes just as I am trying to reconstruct my life. . . . I remember the country that I come from and how it informs my life.*
>
> –Terry Tempest Williams[7]

Africa, the continent, will always be etched into my mind. In my memories, I'll always remember running, playing with other children, and the diversity of food, cultures, and peoples.

At the same time, Africa, in my mind, is also associated with refugees from other East African countries living in the refugee camps in Kenya, the sound of guns and violence looming not too far away, and the molestation that became a norm in my life.

Yet, I also wonder about home. Where is home? How do I find home within myself? My body? Where I live and have lived? And most importantly, where is home with the selves that I've had?

In my journey towards healing, I've also had to ask myself, as other people have asked themselves:

Who am I?
What do I believe?

I am still in the process of answering these questions, but I've learned that I believe in the transformative power of love.

bell hooks, a Black-American writer and theorist writes in her book *All About Love*, "As we love, fear necessarily leaves" (93). Love teaches us to embrace uncertainties. As we love ourselves and others, we wonder: will love be enough? Can love conquer all?

Fear teaches us that anything that is the Other, which is sometimes even ourselves, is worth doubting and rejecting. Love on the other hand asks us to be self-reflective, curious, open and willing.

As the poet Kahlil Gibran writes, "When love beckons to you, follow him, / Though his ways are hard and steep" (15). Choosing the path of love begins with curiosity rather than with fear. From there, the path of love involves accepting the possibility of pain, of being misunderstood, and even grief. The path to love also begins with the self. When you can love yourself, then you can love others.

To My Melanated Skin

The magic didn't fade away with time;
it grew more intense.

Coming Undone

On days that you think your limiting
beliefs are true,
remember how far you've come,
and how much you've survived.

And just like the bud that blossoms with
the passing seasons,
you're growing in ways that you just don't
understand right now.

#Blackgirlmagic

I saw the way we chained our hair,
the way we held them down,
when all they wanted was
to be carefree.

Snapshot: The Therapist's Office

"You have PTSD," the therapist said. He paused and then continued, "You also have schizophrenia."

"What?!"

I was shocked. I felt like I had been coaxed into coming into his office with the possibility of having something "mild" like anxiety or social anxiety disorder. I could accept PTSD, but this diagnosis of schizophrenia was far from what I had expected or wanted in my life.

"No," I repeated, "I don't hear voices and I don't see things."

"I've been through a lot," I said, "Being sexually abused as a child by a neighbor in Kenya really changed everything for me. I think that people are trying to help me. They really care."

He looked at me and said, "Who's they?"

"People."

"What you're experiencing," he said, "is called delusions and ideas of reference."

As time went by, I would learn that I had bipolar disorder and that while my world had changed, it was also expanding.

The First Night

Brick walls,
thickening veins.
I am not the soft person I thought
I'd be.

My Inner Child

"Can you give me the words, mom?"
she said.

I paused.
Looked up.

Gone.

That day,
I realized that I light my own candle.
Shed light onto my wounds.

toxic positivity

"See the silver lining,
smell the freshness after the rain,
find the flower through the thorns," we say.

But what if it's finding the flower *in*
the thorns,
and sitting in the storm,
so that you can feel the pounding, fierceness
of the rain.

What is toxic positivity,
other than a love of productivity,
perfection, and use.
An ideology of
"Be strong"
When that flower is
your wholeness
your humanness.

His first lesson

He cupped the water
gently in his hands,
it trickled down
the gaps in-between his fingers.

His first lesson in love.

Love like untamable water,
Lasting through the gaps,
through the separation of humanness,
of there being a
you and me.

Snapshot: Choosing to Leave

"If you keep coming home late," she told me, "Then you'll need to leave."

I looked at her and said, "But that's not what you said when I was hurting myself. Why can't you be happy for me that I'm happy? Why are you only worried now? Why weren't you worried when I kept trying to hurt myself?"

She looked away.

"Happiness doesn't come from disobeying God," she said, "You can't keep coming home late or you will need to leave."

Reclaiming Myself

So conditioned into the world of
princesses and princes,
the world of
the saved and the savior,
that I forgot my power.

Grief

Grief is an ocean running through
your body.
A wave hits,
you stand back up,
then the other wave comes crashing in.

Some days, grief doesn't come for a visit.
He hides from your laughter,
the things and people you chose,
and is afraid that you've chosen yourself.

To My Therapist

I am the soil that needs
excavating,
before the seed is planted.

Moments when I can swear,
that you're an alchemist
that you took the fire,
and refined me into gold.

I can see now
that I am
the healer,
and the one needing
the healing.

Being A Survivor

"You knew better,"
she says.
"You wanted it,"
she tells me.

Yet as she looms over me,
Shining bright in her cocoon of all-knowingness,
I know that I have stopped believing her.

Self-love

Self-love is knowing that in the unfolding of things,
You are always and will always be favored.

It is the sigh that escaped your lips in the darkest night,
not knowing that
laughter would replace it in the morning.

It is the times you thought,
"Why me?"
Unknown to you that your name and your story
are woven into the fabric of the Earth.

Confronting Your Shadow

When it became clear
that you no longer saw her worth,
her light disappeared,
and you were left with yourself.

Meeting Him

The white Christian man that I love,
the one with the luscious blue eyes
that drip appreciation and awe.

"You've shamed the family,"
you say,
"Brought disgrace to our name."

Rebellious.
Ungrateful.
A slut.

Learning To Breathe

You can unlearn the hardness,
the ways that you've been
taught
being soft
makes you
weak.

Hope

"Their relationship won't last long,"
they said.

But here we are,
well-rooted trees,
holding on strong.

Snapshot: The Absence

"Salam," I say.

"It's you," you say. "Why haven't you called me? When will you visit again? It's been almost a year."

I sigh and think to myself how our calls always center around your need to hear from me. How I should come visit. Yet I rarely call and haven't visited.

"Oh," I say, "I've just been busy. How's everyone doing?"

Three minutes into our call and there's a lull.

I pause, hoping that you'll ask me about him.

"Well, call me when you're free," you say.

"Okay," I say. "*ma'salama* and tell everyone I said *salam*."

love's lantern

Love is like a glass lantern placed in a river;
it shines brighter on the darkest nights.

Sometimes, that lantern glides smoothly,
no bumps, no pressure,
pure rapture.

On other days,
love's lantern sways furiously through the river of life,
where the grass, the birds, and all of creation whisper
a prayer for you.

morality police

Like rabid dogs,
Men will tear you into pieces in
the comments,
and then slide into your DMs.
for a treat.

Some days,
they're ranting about that sister—
the lost cause.

A round of applause, please,
for our morality police.

The Somali That's Gone Bad

Shorts, tank tops, margaritas,
holding a man's head in my lap as we laugh,
singing along at Church with the worship music.

These days, I still read Hafiz, Rumi
and ways of softening my heart.
I still burn *unsi*,[8]
Paint paintings of women in *hijab*.

Beyond Forms

Your chosen path,
Might not fit the frame that you had.

You tried cutting the edges,
realized that you lost your personal touch.

You tried getting another frame,
until the light trickled in.

Nothing can contain you.

Letters from My Partner

A Desert Rose in Bloom
by Mitchell Gordon

The vibrant colors stood in a dusty scene,
Such a harsh land, yet it had not left its mark on the petals.
The rose seemed unaffected by the dry and dusty land around it,
it stood strong, true, and firm,
gracing the scene in its beauty.

The desert needed the rose,
Just as much as the rose needed the desert.
Together,
Their beauty was made even more spectacular.

Many questioned it,
Few understood it,
But all who witnessed it,
Appreciated it and felt its worth.

The rose was self-sufficient
Hold on to the water the sky released
Sustaining what was given far beyond other roses.

The roots of the rose were true,
Firm and deep.
The petals of the rose were soft, moist, and vibrant,
Leaving a hue,
Not quite seen before.

When sun would set and rise,
It would dance off the rose,
Leaving feelings of
Peace, comfort and warmth.

Accountability Meets Growth
by Mitchell Gordon

That smile,
Where did it go?

Is it in the darkest place?
Lower than the low?

If happiness is a choice,
Why did you put it there?

It used to come freely, natural
With its flow.
Now it is bent, broken and slow.

The more power you give them,
The more that they take,
So much so that
smile becomes masked.

Your natural ability to shine and glisten,
Can all return,
When the right souls will listen.

Notes

1 See Bessel A. van der Kolk, *The Body Keeps the Score: Brain, Mind, and Body in the Healing of Trauma* (New York: Penguin, 2014).

2. *Eid* translates to "holiday" in Arabic, while *Imama* is a May-May / Somali term for a headwrap worn by Muslim men.

3. Used in the Somali language to say "bye." The literal meaning in Arabic is "with peace."

4. "Father" in the May-May language.

5. See Judith Butler, *Gender Trouble: Feminism and the Subversion of Identity* (New York: Routledge, 2006).

6. A historical Somali queen that stands as a cultural icon for feminism.

7. Terry Tempest Williams, "Prologue," *Refuge: An Unnatural History of Family and Place*, 2nd Vintage Books ed. (New York: Vintage, 2001), 3.

8. Somali for "incense."

Bibliography

Butler, Judith. *Gender Trouble: Feminism and the Subversion of Identity.* New York: Routledge, 2006.

Gibran, Kahlil. *The Prophet.* New York: Alfred A. Knopf, 1923.

hooks, bell. *All About Love: New Visions.* New York: HarperCollins, 2001.

Perry, Bruce D., and Oprah Winfrey. *What Happened to You?: Conversations on Trauma, Resilience, and Healing.* New York: Flatiron Books, 2021.

Van der Kolk, Bessel. *The Body Keeps the Score: Brain, Mind and Body in the Healing of Trauma.* New York: Penguin Books, 2014.

Williams, Terry Tempest. *Refuge: An Unnatural History of Family and Place.* 1992. 2nd Vintage Books ed. New York: Vintage, 2001.

Acknowledgments

I would like to thank my partner, Mitchell Gordon, and our family for their support. I would also like to thank Sahna Foley, Vince Font, the Asian Association of Utah, and all the amazing people in my life who have made this possible. Much thanks to Dr. Ross Tangedal and Cornerstone Press for believing in this book.

Gratefully acknowledged are the following publications, where particular pieces first appeared:

"Snapshot: The Departure and Arrival", "Snapshot: 9/11 and Racial Passing", and "Snapshot: The Therapist's Office" were originally published by the Blended Futures Project as a single essay titled "Fault Lines", 7 October 2021.

"Becoming the Moon" was originally published in *Diaspora Baby Blues*, Winter 2020–2021.

Takwa (Tee) Gordon is a Somali-American writer, editor, and social worker. She holds an MA in English and minors in comparative literature and literacy. She enjoys painting, running, reading, and kayaking. She currently lives in Ogden, Utah with her family.

www.ingramcontent.com/pod-product-compliance
Lightning Source LLC
Chambersburg PA
CBHW030309100526
44590CB00012B/570